I0893532

WEIRD AND UNUSUAL ANIMALS

FLYING DRAGONS

by Karen Latchana Kenney

AMICUS HIGH INTEREST • AMICUS INK

Amicus High Interest and
Amicus Ink are imprints of Amicus
P.O. Box 1329, Mankato, MN 56002
www.amicuspublishing.us

Library of Congress Cataloging-in-Publication Data
Names: Kenney, Karen Latchana, author.
Title: Flying Dragons / by Karen Latchana Kenney.
Description: Mankato, Minnesota : Amicus, 2018. | Series: Weird and unusual animals | Includes index. | Audience: Grades K to 3.
Identifiers: LCCN 2016042395 (print) | ISBN 9781681511566 (library binding) | ISBN 9781681521879 (pbk.) | ISBN 9781681512464 (ebook)
Subjects: LCSH: Draco (Reptiles)--Juvenile literature.
Classification: LCC QL666.L223 K46 2017 (print) | DDC 597.95/5--dc23
LC record available at https://lccn.loc.gov/2016042395

Photo Credits: tets/Shutterstock background pattern; Victor Tan/Singapore/Flickr cover; Tim MacMillan/John Downer Pro/Nature Picture Library/Alamy Stock Photo 2; A.S.Kono/WikiCommons 4–5; Stephen Dalton/Nature Picture Library/Alamy Stock Photo 7; B_Y_N_G/iStock 8–9; Matthieu Berroneau/France & Australia/Flickr 10–11; shikheigoh/RooM the Agency/Alamy Stock Photo 12; Sarah Tahourdin of Auscape International Pty Ltd/Australia 14–15; kurt_G/Shutterstock 16–17; NHPA/NHPA/Superstock 18–19; Ganesh H Shankar/Alamy Stock Photo 20; Premaphotos/Alamy Stock Photo 22

Editor: Wendy Dieker
Designer: Aubrey Harper
Photo Researcher: Holly Young

Printed in the United States of America

HC 10 9 8 7 6 5 4 3 2 1
PB 10 9 8 7 6 5 4 3 2 1

TABLE OF CONTENTS

A QUICK ESCAPE

A lizard sits on a branch. A hungry snake slides toward it. The lizard opens its wings. Jump! The snake is surprised! The flying dragon glides away to safety.

GLIDING LIZARD

The flying dragon is not a dragon. And it doesn't really fly. Its wings catch the wind like a kite. It can glide up to 30 feet (9 m). It uses its long tail to steer.

Weird but True

A flying dragon has another name. It is also called a Draco lizard.

8

TREE DWELLER

The flying dragon is found in the **jungles** of Southeast Asia. It lives in trees. It rarely goes to the ground. It gets around by gliding between the trees.

Weird but True

A flying dragon is small. It only grows to be about 8 inches (20 cm) long.

BUG HUNTER

Bugs are everywhere in the jungle's trees. Ants and termites are the flying dragon's favorite food. The lizard sits and waits on a branch. A bug comes close. Snatch! The lizard grabs it.

FOLDS OF SKIN

The flying dragon has extra folds of skin. The skin stretches between a set of long **ribs** to make wings. Extra skin is on its neck, too. This is the flying dragon's **dewlap**.

Weird but True

A male's dewlap is bright yellow. A female's is not as bright. It might be blue or other colors.

COLOR DANCE

A male is looking for a **mate**. He circles a female. He shows his colorful wings. His colorful dewlap sticks out. The female sees the male's bright colors. She likes his dance.

DRAGON EGGS

A female goes to the ground to lay eggs. She finds moist dirt and makes a hole. She lays up to five eggs. Then she covers the eggs with dirt.

Weird but True

The mother never sees her babies. She leaves the eggs before they hatch.

ON GUARD

Each male flying dragon has a **territory**. One male lives in a few trees. He guards his space fiercely. He glides to chase other males away. Other males watch out!

Weird but True
More than one female lives in a territory.

20

BLENDING IN

A flying dragon can glide away from danger. It can also hide from enemies. It tucks away its wings. The lizard blends into the tree bark. Can you see it?

A LOOK AT FLYING DRAGONS

WORDS TO KNOW

dewlap – a flap of skin on a flying dragon's neck

jungle – an area of land with many trees, vines, and bushes in warm parts of the world

mate – a male or female partner in an animal pair

ribs – curved bones on an animal's chest; flying dragons have a set of extra long ribs that move to open their wings.

territory – the area under control of an animal

LEARN MORE

Books

Collard, Sneed B. *Catching Air: Taking the Leap with Gliding Animals*. Thomaston, Maine: Tilbury House Publishers, 2017.

Marsh, Laura. *Lizards*. Washington, DC: National Geographic Society, 2012.

Websites

Easy Science for Kids, Flying Dragons or Draco Lizards—The Lizards That Can Fly
http://easyscienceforkids.com/all-about-flying-dragons

Wild Kratts, All About Lizards
www.pbs.org/parents/wildkratts/activities/all-about-lizards

INDEX